origami heart

Poems by a Woman Doing Life

erin george

BleakHouse Publishing

2009

origami heart

Poems by a Woman Doing Life

By
erin george

COVER ART
francesca george

COVER DESIGN
elizabeth calka

TEXT DESIGN
sonia tabriz

BleakHouse Publishing

2009

www.bleakhousepublishing.com

Copyright © 2009 by Erin George

All rights reserved. No part of this book shall be reproduced or transmitted in any form or by any means, electronic, mechanical, magnetic, photographic including photocopying, recording or by any information storage and retrieval system, without prior written permission of the publisher. No patent liability is assumed with respect to the use of the information contained herein. Although every precaution has been taken in the preparation of this book, the publisher and author assume no responsibility for errors or omissions. Neither is any liability assumed for damages resulting from the use of the information contained herein.

ISBN-13: 978-0-9797065-5-4
ISBN-10:   0-9797065-5-6

BleakHouse Publishing

NEC Box 67
New England College
Henniker, New Hampshire 03242
www.BleakHousePublishing.com

To my Jack, Fran, and Gio:
Love you, love you more, love you most...
Got you!

And to my parents –
no thank you can ever be enough

ACKNOWLEDGMENTS

It's difficult for any poet to find her voice, much less someone willing to listen. This is especially true when the poet is incarcerated. But I've been blessed to discover people to help me accomplish both. I'd like to thank Turtle Tibbs, who brought me to my first poetry class, and Amanda McRaven, who taught that class. Another of my teachers was Paul Priest, who every week shared his vast knowledge and love of poetry with me, constantly encouraging me to hone my work. I'm also grateful to Susan Williamson and Sharon Leiter of Streetlight Magazine and Susan Nagelsen of New England College for their encouragement. Most of all, I thank Robert Johnson, who has become a friend and mentor. Without him, this book would never have been published.

TABLE OF CONTENTS

Origami Heart ♥ 1

Cloistered ♥ 3

First Time ♥ 4

Oblation ♥ 5

Captured Sky ♥ 7

Pastoral ♥ 8

My Father's Chair ♥ 9

Lost Love ♥ 10

Before the Kiln ♥ 11

Inevitability ♥ 12

Defenestration ♥ 13

Elementary Juju ♥ 14

Frustration ♥ 15

Cano ♥ 16

The Letter I Can Never Write ♥ 17

A Lover's Plea ♥ 19

Mere Haiku ♥ 20

My Kimono ♥ 21

Night Song ♥ 22

Nurturing Opals ♥ 23

Panacea ♥ 24

Patchwork Man ♥ 25

Summer Twilights ♥ 26

True Love ♥ 27

Vacancies ♥ 28

Venus Of Willendorf ♥ 29

Walking Through The Woods ♥ 30

Reflections From A Prison Yard ♥ 31

Wanderings ♥ 32

With Due Respect To Randall Jarrell ♥ 33

Microcosm ♥ 34

Galatea ♥ 35

Forbidden Words ♥ 36

A Poem For My Mother ♥ 37

(For Jack) ♥ 38

Undoing Time ♥ 39

Bapa's Ring ♥ 41

The Perfection Of The Arm ♥ 42

Bluebeard's Seventh Wife ♥ 43

Narcissus ♥ 44

The Selkie ♥ 45

Mastering Grief ♥ 46

Phantom Limb ♥ 47

Leonid Shower ♥ 48

Life Sentence ♥ 49

First Time, Defenestration, Frustration, Patchwork Man, Vacancies, With Due Respect to Randall Jarrell, Undoing Time, and The Selkie are reprinted with permission from Exiled Voices *(New England College Press 2008).*

erin george

ORIGAMI HEART

I can see how carefully
you always fold your letters,
intricate layers of notebook paper,
compact,
like a note you might slip
to a friend in class,
hidden in cupped palms

or push through the vents
of some boy's locker,
too shy for anything more overt.

When I pick them up at mail call
I feel them slide back and forth
in the flimsy blue and red striped
airmail envelopes,
a core of your words
and so much emptiness enclosed.

Sometimes I let myself imagine
that the empty space
still contains your air,
the envelope a lung
breathing out the same
uncomplicated, milky sweetness
I remember from before,
when I could hold you.

You would reach up
and stroke my earlobe
with your thumb
to lull yourself to sleep.

As I inhaled you,
your fingers were as soft
as felt

origami heart

as soft as the creases
in your letters
after my manifold readings –
soft, threatening severance,
but still holding.

CLOISTERED

Bowed with the weight
of my manacles
I enter a house of penitence.

My hair carelessly shorn
and my possessions stripped,
I am a novice in a mendicant order.

My new uniform of raw burgundy
stains my skin
with false stigmata.

Morning headcount is my matins,
evening lockdown is my vespers,
and the hours in between
marked not by counted bells
but by dictates hurled
from clamorous loudspeakers.

I am the bride of no one now
but will abide here in my cell,
a stony niche
in a two-tiered columbarium
until I return to ashes.

origami heart

FIRST TIME

I don't remember your hands.

Rough, gentle, I can't say which.
I can't remember any pain
and my memory is soundless.
Here is what I do remember:

The lunar surface of the garage floor,
cold and gray as a morgue,
pitted against my salty cheek.

My fingers twisting, greasy
in the square of oil-spattered green shag
crudely hacked from your old bedroom carpeting.

The band of hiked-up nightgown,
knotted and thick as an umbilical cord,
pressing against my stomach.

The cave of cobwebs and suspended fly corpses
under your workbench,
my only focus.

You, afterwards, washing my favorite panties,
the ones with My Pretty Pony on them,
in the seldom-used utility sink,
promising repercussions and ice cream.

OBLATION
For Francesca

Your first night home
you and I lie half asleep
in the tree-filtered moonlight
of our muted apartment
at three a.m., the softest hour.

We are cocooned
within the well-sprung sofa,
our bare skin scratched
by the crocheted afghan
I've wrapped around us.

Lulled by your waning pulls,
I contemplate our shared sacraments,
truer than any *pro forma* rite.

First, the bloody wash of your baptism,
when you slipped from me
wizened and red-daubed
as an ochered shaman.
Your silent arrival
summoned anxious doctors
like a star.

Next, those six long days
in N.I.C.U.,
your pale body
enormous next to hand-span
crack babies
twitching unvisited
under warming lights.

Well-scrubbed as a surgeon
I was allowed to finally hold you,
tethered by coils of clear plastic tubing

origami heart

anchored with large-bore needles
in your fleshless hands and feet,
stigmatized by blown I.V. sites
and striated with remnants
of greyed tape adhesive.
Anointing you with tears
I inventoried your wounds
and inscribed them in my heart.

Then finally we could take you home,
beyond the mandatory cheer
of the pediatric ward
and the grim auguries
gauzed in sympathy.

Now, in the half-light
we share our quiet communion
and I know that you are whole.
The even suction of your mouth
against my breast
compels not just simple nourishment
but the transubstantiation
of my milk
into the essence of our covenant,
mingling me inside you
in a profound and welcome bondage.

erin george

CAPTURED SKY

A photo album full of sky:
glossy, white-framed echoes
of weekend flights
in my father's two-seat Cessna

memories trapped by my camera,
cobalt blue plastic
bumpered with black rubber,
its broad, textured buttons
perfect for my clumsy hands.

I'd never waste my film
on the terrestrial:
just endless shots
of clarity and clouds
and slivers of silver wing

capturing the best part
of those crystal afternoons
we shared.

PASTORAL

The snap of tattered jonquil sheet
and its slow petal descent
over sere August lawn
was our Sunday summer ritual.

I was an eager picnicker,
but not for any great love
of sun-crusted ham sandwiches
or the cups of neglected lemonade,
irresistible as a pitcher plant,
full of tiny deaths.

I relished the give,
that satisfying crunch
of desiccated grass
beneath the frayed cotton
whenever I pressed down.

Heady with a six-year-old's omnipotence
I clambered between the paper plates
flecked with translucence
like Godzilla
searching for new cities to scourge
until my mother's rebuke
conquered me.

Veneered with obedience
I retreated
to my flattened patch of sod
but the gravid crackle
was still cupped
in my smudged palm,
enveloped like a secret.

MY FATHER'S CHAIR

Low and deep
Is my father's chair,
Eternal and round as an *omphalos*,
Hazed by his Glenfidditch aura
And girt by the world:
History, science, philosophy, and literature
In untidy pillars encolumn it.
His habits and topography
Have engraved a graticule
Of rendings in the smoky leather,
His own Turin winding sheet
Confirming his existence.

LOST LOVE

The engraving inside my wedding band
is almost gone now,
worn by lovers' hands.

I can still make out a year,
1920,
if I catch the sun just right

but her name is lost to me
as are any attendant declarations,
and I have no one left to ask.

erin george

BEFORE THE KILN

In your newness
you are as soft as kaolin
before the kiln

still moist
from a Jiangxi mountain,
waiting for my shaping
and time's heat
to finalize you.

For now you are a simple form,
like a bowl
of Sung Dynasty porcelain

eggshell white
with an underglaze of blue
your unadorned curves
filled with cries and possibilities.

INEVITABILITY

How preposterous you are
with your soft lolling head
swaying on a neck
as tender and tenuous
as a mung bean sprout.

When I first hold you
the old wives' tale seems entirely plausible,
that babies are reaped
from under a cabbage leaf,
fruit of some bizarre parthenogenesis.

I mean, look at you:
crumpled and pale from your long furling,
damp as garden mold
and utterly organic in your wants.

How is it, then, that you,
my cherished abstraction
so improbably realized,
you, with your invertebrate flailings
and inchoate seekings
induce a symbiosis as inevitable
as your being?

erin george

DEFENESTRATION

When I was seven
my sister and I
orchestrated our escape.
Kicking through the rusted flyscreen,
meant to keep things out, not in,
we hurled ourselves like B'rer Rabbit
into the thicket of boxwood below,
then glad-footed careened
across the sun-sharp grass
'til our trajectories were thwarted
by a heedful babysitter
who had pried herself away
from telephone and TV set
long enough to glimpse us
cannonball past the kitchen window.

Now my window to the world
is 5x40 inches,
a sliver of normality
absurdly Constable in its composition:
a pond parasolled by contorted oak
a slew of bold and bickering geese
and in the distance, a bijou farmhouse,
all this framed by flaking cinderblock
and fingernail scarred putty,
gouged with tiny excavations
and thick-furred with neglect.
No child's begrimed feet
can force an exit here.
The passage is too narrow.

ELEMENTARY JUJU

You waterfall down
the ridged rubber steps
of the school bus
into the grey November cold,
your Power Rangers backpack
dangling from one shoulder
like a cat-snapped wing,
a torrent of words and feet
tangling in your eagerness.

When we finally get inside the house
you explain with all the gravitas
a six-year old can muster
that now you know the trick,
a super-secret way to make it snow.

It's a very special magic
you say with breathless import,
sure to bring at least a foot of snow.

As I make maternal peeps of encouragement
you demonstrate the elaborate moves involved –
an awkward dance
of sways and spins and waves.

When your magic's finally done
you tell me what you want to do
when your snow comes:
build a fort, and sled with Bryan,
and make some snow ice cream.
And I smile, and smile, and smile,
as I pray silently for snow.

FRUSTRATION
For Lana S.

In my cell
affixed chest high
are four gunmetal steel hooks
hinged as prophylactics
against despair

can't hang my bathrobe
or myself

CANO

I sing of the arms of my man*
as hot around me as a Carthage night
and heavy with unmet promises

I splayed my wealth before him,
a queen's ransom
offered to a sea-skipping wanderer

He tasted the gold of my coins
and I swooned
as his teeth made contact

He fingered my treasures
like some canny merchant,
and I let him

But the only thing he gave me
was the boot,
and now I am alone

My pyre on the shore
is a beacon,
but he's turned his eyes away

It calls to me, though,
and like an intoxicated bee
I stumble in, insensate

* *"Arma virumque cano" ("I sing of arms and a man") – first line of Virgil's Aenead*

erin george

THE LETTER I CAN NEVER WRITE

My Darling Jack
My Precious Fran
My Gio, oh, my joy!

I write electroplated letters every week,
cankerous truth swathed
in false furbelows
that are my gifts to you

I tell of the flowerbeds,
scattered tokens of springtime,
whose growth I mark as faithfully
as on the pantry door
I once charted yours
(a blue line for Jack,
pink for Francesca,
and Gio's colors changing with her whims)
but never mention
that I'm not permitted near enough
to test their fragrance

You hear of my visits
with Grandma and Bapa,
the snacks we ate,
the news we shared,
but never, never, my debasement afterward,
stripped of my scrubs and my dignity
squatting clumsy as a troglodyte,
lifting milk-scarred breasts
for possible concealments,
opening my mouth for inspection
like a knackered mare

origami heart

I write of friends not really had
and comforts all untrue –
I can't do anything for you from here
but armor you from my reality

In fact, the only verity
in all my words,
the only message
untainted in my bowdlerized epistles
is I love you.

I love you.
I love you.
I love you.

A LOVER'S PLEA

Save your soft moth touches
for some dream-struck girl.
I want reality.

Brand me
with black haloes
round my eyes.

Daub me
with your sanguine
fingerpaints.

Stake your claim
with rose-stitched
cowboy boots.

Prove to me
I'm yours.
Make me real.

MERE HAIKU
For Paul Priest

I am mere haiku
a fleck of an idea
in chained syllables

scraps of poetry
wrought in petalled unfurlings
bloom pink inside me

dewed with an attar
compounded in lonely hours
myself poured inward.

MY KIMONO

The night is my kimono.
Silked within its plummy heart
is a patterned flurry
of moth wings
unpinned from velvet moorings.

Sashless in its concealments,
damascened through lunar alchemy,
I am not delved by observation
but open to the laving tongues
of demure chrysanthemum breeze.

NIGHT SONG
For Sylvia Plath

She listens through the walls
to her son's wails,
torpid in 200 thread count sheets
this termite queen in a flowered shroud from Sak's
a statue in a moon-trapped square
Galatea not yet loved.

Her Irish linen nightgown, convent-embellished, balloons
slow over her nakedness
as the notes of her son's cry
try to reel her in,
a hook through the ear
next to a diamond stud,
not too big, but tasteful.

She unwraps inside her head
an unrequested Mother's Day gift
(can't be returned like those tacky wineglasses)
and visualizing her son's seeking hand
where succor can't be found
she can almost rise

but her elements are too fractured,
gulfweed tangles in her own Sargasso Sea
with no rescue plane in sight.
She's been undone by expectations
and no diminishing night song is enough
to make her coalesce.

NURTURING OPALS

I always loved the opals best,
those shards of hummingbird
caged by Victorian gold,
snared by a tangle
of yellowed pearls
in the blue moiré hollow
of my grandmother's tall
tiered jewelry box.

Opals were unique
she told me
because you have to care for them
or they will die,
caress them in oil
or they grow brittle
and shatter at rough treatment.

Hearing this I wondered
how it could be
that all this prismed fragility
could survive the unattending earth
so long without us.

PANACEA

On her deep kitchen windowsill
my mother had an aloe vera plant,
flat-leaved and arcing in its terra-cotta pot

surrounded by the domestic detritus of our life
(a battered cup full of sticky pennies
and lockless keys,
ignored correspondence too important to misplace,
a sun-spangled row of pebbles
deemed jewels by a toddler's appraisal).

Whenever I suffered
some small calamity of childhood
she would snap off the tip
of one succulent lobe

(no matter how often she did
it never grew less lush –
when I finally left home
it had outgrown its sunny spot)

and take its unguent sap
to soothe me with her balming hands.
"There," she would say,
"doesn't that feel better now?"

PATCHWORK MAN

He read my body like Braille,
too simple for him to decipher.
Where I wrote runes,
he found roadmaps
and arrows saying
"You are here."

I carry pieces of him with me,
so without protracted searching
I find that place where my tongue fits
just behind his ear
lapping up his alchemical, sweat-rendered syrup.

I still stumble on his clutter,
a thicket of cleats and clubs and cricket bats
and cursing, reel to see him
smirking at the discord he has sown.

I taste the clumsy meal,
uneaten then but savored now,
he prepared to comfort me,
soul-sick over our lost child.

He's more than just some APB rundown:
Brown hair, blue eyes, no distinguishing marks.
James is an amalgam of contradictions
hoarded in me like a Saxon trove.

I fuse the scattered facets of my love:
His knack for guessing birthday gifts,
the way he'd dangle Gio as she chortled,
the yin and yang of his contrition and his ire.

I assemble these within to make my quilt
while coldly I lie longing in my bed.
My construct is not near enough to truth,
but will undimming live as long as I.

SUMMER TWILIGHTS

I

We flew like bats
through the teeming twilight,
loping through moonrise,
snatching amorous fireflies
from their slow, sparking semaphore
and hoarding them
in clouded Mason jars,
a trove of Tinkerbells.

II

Obscured by deep pansy dusk
we took our lightning bug booty
and stole their sparks,
their voices,
and bedecked ourselves
with their snipped luminescence,
fairy rings
with a half-life of moments
but endlessly replaceable.

We know no better.

TRUE LOVE

A chiaroscuro study
rendered in the wedge
of door-funneled bathroom light

Her anemone fingers whisper
tousled motel sheets
over dappled, yeasty breasts,
Andromeda chained
in constellated fingertip bruises

The percussion of abandonment
overlays the scene,
the chink of his belt buckle,
a sheathed cascade of pocket change,
crescendo with the lonely chatter
of unlocking chain and deadbolt,
then closing click
unsoftened by goodbye

VACANCIES

I suffer from a superfluity
of lap

not needed
as a makeshift cradle
now

nor used
as comforter
for weeping child.

Yes, I suffer,
but perhaps
my malady

is more accurately
diagnosed
as an excess of absence.

VENUS OF WILLENDORF

The arc of the Earth
echoes in your
breasts
belly
thighs

Woman pared to essentials

Fräulein,
you are four-and-a-half inches of
Paleolithic
procreative
dynamite

WALKING THROUGH THE WOODS

Most days are like a trail of breadcrumbs
dropped with ponderous regularity
on the path leading in,
unglanced at and presumed
waiting for the reconnection

until, finally turning,
you find them gone,
snapped down the gullets
of selfish thrushes,
speckled brown as the forest floor
or pilfered
by a funereal procession
of brittle black ants.

Poor choice!
Better would have been
smooth white pebbles
to cast off the moon's light.
You can find pockets full
if you pay attention.

Their small weight,
like a handful of hummingbird eggs,
is warmed thoroughly
by your palm.

erin george

REFLECTIONS FROM A PRISON YARD

One would imagine
as we stand
in the treeless autumn
of the prison yard,
our eyes snared
by the basso profundo declarations
from the skein of geese overhead
that we envy them
their utter freedom,
their strong-breasted flights
with unclipped wings.

Really, though,
we all just wish
we were having roast goose
for dinner.

WANDERINGS

After my mom made me
turn off the lights at bedtime
I would travel.

In the tented stifle
of my sheets and blankets
I would click on my yellow flashlight,
casting its gold corona
to gather from L'Engle, Bradbury, or Lewis
provision for my wanderings.

Later, heady from deep draughts
of dandelion wine
and the fragrance of Aslan's mane
I would close my book
and do my own chronicling,
my hands making shadowed glyphs
against the white cotton
as I recast the story,

almost forgotten by morning
but at night, at night
as evocative as runes,
transforming my canopy of bedclothes
into my own time machine
and place machine
and everlasting dream machine.

erin george

WITH DUE RESPECT TO RANDALL JARRELL*

I also fell into the State.
Not its belly, but its bowels,
clenched and shaking like a fist
inside a basement holding cell.
My sentence was not douched oblivion.
It was life, bacterial,
until rehabilitation does me in.

*A response to his "The Death of the Bull Turret Gunner"

MICROCOSM

Consider

the whelk perfection
of your infant daughter's hand
as it lies luminous
in the patterned moonlight
of her crib.

God is in these details

GALATEA

Stumbling from the plinth
onto his workshop floor
her unlined feet
uncoil crimson threads
around the drift of ivory splinters,
a torturous matting,
and the pain consumes
the last fragmented memory

of arcing low over the savannah
skimming brown yellow grey green
swells of dry expanse,
prow to a grass-fueled schooner
mapping sun-speared wanderings
in an endless vegetative search

only knowing love
as splintering lust-spurred conflict
over grey maidens

until that foam-born jade's animation
propelled her dazed
into an arid sea
of counterfeit passion,
a pale avatar of delight
doomed to bloodless couplings
and a man's shaggy fist.

FORBIDDEN WORDS

Each inmate has a secret vocabulary
that can only be whispered after lockdown,
a litany too evocative to bear casual invocation.

Franny, Gio, Jack and James,
your grandmother's engagement ring,
that old oak bed we bought...
a quiver full of the lost
that sieve me like St. Sebastian.

The profane is boldly spoken here,
a patois steeped in barbarism.
The words with real power we keep sheathed
except in calculated measures,
a prison homeopathy
vaccinating against a wasting sickness.

erin george

A POEM FOR MY MOTHER

Restless with fever
I crawled into my mother's bed
before her alarm clock rang.

In the sacheted dimness
her cool, appraising hand
against my hot stomach
anchored me under the duvet
so that stillness could come
and I could hear more
than just my agued brain.

After her ministry
of juice and St. Joseph's
she would sing to me
in her mother-perfect voice
until the room spanned dark to light

singing the Mills Brothers'
"Glow Little Glow Worm,"
as I do for my daughter now,
singing until my cool, affixing hand
can bring her rest.

(FOR JACK)

I died in childbirth.

the I
the Me
any part I played in We
subsumed

the bone-displacing grindings
of your birth
reincarnated Me
in the You
and the He

erin george

UNDOING TIME

We are a prison of Penelopes
so busy at our looms
so full of weavings and unweavings

the strangling weft and warp
is plucked into dirging thrum
like fretful catgut
by our lanolinned fingers
greasy from the unwashed
wool we use, undyed,
grey as the ashes
of an apocalyptic sun

we're so busy
under official daylight eyes
dumb as sheep
bleating yessir, yessir
in our ungreen Ithaca.

We are equally busy in the night
dismantling our work,
using our teeth if necessary,
unpicking inches like reversed time
the tumorous wool
uneven as stacked hourglasses,
unusable for tomorrows.

We snip it into tiny lengths
and fling it away
in a ghastly nocturnal tickertape parade
celebrating one more dodging
of a resolution,
some unknown quota
still unreached
because unreachings
are unendings

origami heart

and it's conclusions
that we dread,
conclusions with their hafted
denouements that set us
weaving and unweaving
to begin with.

BAPA'S RING
For my father, For my son

The gold was almost gone,
pilfered by decades,
a black bas-relief of Athena
held tenuously in the vulnerable circle,
its engraving almost brushed away
by time and circumstance.

And on it went,
from father to father
until you,
with your knack for the redemptive,
took it in hand
and strengthened it again
with your own gold,
preparing it for the next.

origami heart

THE PERFECTION OF THE ARM

We are different,
we women,
beyond the obvious
pink petal show.

It's there, within
the white orchid blossom
of our pelvis,
a fecund, night-blooming
lepidoptera flare

and in the perfection
of our arm
arced as subtle
as the horizon,
an osseous cradle
ideal for its burdens.

Inside ourselves we are like
the earth.
We are designed to carry life.

erin george

BLUEBEARD'S SEVENTH WIFE

See this fat heart
in rich enameled casket,
my wrenched offering
damply sheened in its bright box
like an unwithered relic
still recognizable as itself.

It was not the first
in your collection
and I let you take it
knowing of all the others
drained and dangling
in your darkness,
pendant white wax dollies

the *hush hush* of their slow spins
slide under all your words
but don't prevent me
from unlocking that narrow door.

NARCISSUS

I fall into the pond,
falling into that dark mouth
so full of unseen life.

It happens in an instant,
my falling,
but I cannot resist it
sitting on the splintered dock
in my yellow bathing suit
with the snappy red straps.

I can't resist
the dim world
wavering under water
like the fairytale,
but instead of sheep
there is a house
like my house,
only vague where mine is solid
(and, I infer, concrete where mine dissolves)
and doppelgänger tree-tangled moon
bright as my sister's St. Agnes spoon,
kept in a glass box on her dresser,
a baptismal gift
useful only for feeding air
to a nursery of bland plastic faces.

My falling is irrevocable,
without companion rising,
my falling into that dark mouth
so full of precipitate death.

erin george

THE SELKIE
For Gio

You are unabashedly unpeeled,
bathing suit a tangled
sandy splatter,
a polychrome abandonment
spilled just beyond
the high tide's boundary
of shattered shells
and clumps of black-brown kelp.

Your bright plastic pail is forgotten.
Instead, your sleek, sea-dark head
bends low as you painstakingly
decipher a sandpiper's
circling cuneiform.

Your own meanderings,
a chain of footprints
washed to phocidic wedges,
could just as easily lead from
as to the sea.
I can't be sure,
seeing you pick your way
among black rocks,
your raw pink kinesis
constrained by uncertain footing.

Are you yourself, my girl,
or some fey creature
seeking her stolen sealskin
to slip it on and slip away from me
between the green strata
of the sun-warmed sea?

MASTERING GRIEF

The mastery of grief
starts with your thousandth paper crane
wishes strung together like a garland.

At first it seems insurmountable
but the stark geometry of the task
slices through every vagueness
until each fold is mastered
and the feel of the paper,
as smooth and cool as an indifferent glance,
is as familiar as his touch.

At last it is done,
grief settled in like a possessive lover,
twined within sinews, propelling you
through a mimicry of life

yet in a forgotten room
the covies of cranes hang unfading,
clustered like dementing fruit.
Each time the door is opened
they brush together uneasily,
murmuring regrets.

PHANTOM LIMB

Through the spell of half-awareness
his arm still echoes
in the valley of your waist

it lingers, welcome anchor
in the turbulence of bedclothes,
the confusion of sleep's
near drownings

you feel that familiar arm:
bowler of a wicked googly,
hefter of brown paper grocery bags,
cradler of your commingling

you feel it
the way an amputee
still feels what is lost,
the insatiable itch and ache
as real and unprovable as God

you feel it
until remembrance comes,
not with the slow evanescence
of placid awakenings
but with the instant scalpel clarity
of ruthless light

and the comforter's weight is just
a slippery heap of satin
shoddily stitched by strangers' hands

you feel it
slide heavily to the floor
as you begin to rise,
leaving you naked and abandoned
to the present

origami heart

LEONID SHOWER

At 2:00 a.m.
we all gathered in the front yard
in the spring dark cold
with arms full of old quilts
drooping like a bouquet
of tattered peonies.

Shannon had come,
and between us we brought
the little ones downstairs,
still in their footie pajamas,
uncomprehending in their drowse,
and nestled them in blankets
on the night-damp grass.

We murmured to each other
as we learned to see in darkness,
waiting for the first movement of light.

When at last I saw a slow flash
arcing just over the cottonwoods
I touch Francesca beneath our shared quilt
to show her where to look,
her small flannelled body
warm beside me.

At the next brief streak
she silently grabbed my hand,
not letting go again
until the sky was full of light.

LIFE SENTENCE
For Jennifer, convicted at age 16

A bevy of images accompany her
like bridesmaids trailing a jilted bride.

I see her as she's meant to be:
flamboyantly saronged,
curling brown toes in sea-packed sand,
remnants of a billion years' abrasions.
The ambient gold of liquid sun
glazes her like caramelized sugar.

I see her as she has become:
too exposed and unadorned,
ill-fitted to her prison scrubs.
The chemical fluorescent light
of the day room
steals her hues.

Jennifer consists of contrasts,
warring facets of a single gem.
Her cabochon heart erodes
between prison's relentless gears
until her faces smooth
to one diminished grain of sand,
a bland patina secreting nacred core.

ABOUT THE AUTHOR

Erin George *(Author)* neither read nor wrote poetry prior to joining a prison writers' group in 2003. Since then, her work has appeared in several magazines and has been included in an anthology of prison work titled "Exiled Voices" (New England College Press, 2008). She also won First Place in the PEN Prison Poetry Competition in 2006 and currently is at work on a memoir of her prison experiences.

ABOUT THE ARTISTS

Francesca George *(Cover Art)* was born in Washington, D.C. on November 29, 1996. She is a student at The Royal Masonic School for Girls in Hertfordshire, England.

Elizabeth Calka *(Cover Design)* is an undergraduate student at American University majoring in Visual Media and minoring in Graphic Design. She also is a photographer and poet, as well as the main architect of the Bleakhouse Publishing website.

Sonia Tabriz *(Text Design)* is an undergraduate student at American University majoring in Law & Society and Psychology. She is a published author of fiction as well as an artist. Tabriz is the Editor-In-Chief of *Tacenda Literary Magazine* and the Managing Editor of BleakHouse Publishing.

BleakHouse Publishing
NEC Box 67
New England College
Henniker, New Hampshire 03242
www.BleakHousePublishing.com

PUBLISHER
Melissa Lang

EDITOR
Robert Johnson

MANAGING EDITORS
Susan Nagelsen
Sonia Tabriz

CONSULTING EDITORS
Rachel Cupelo
Christopher Dum
Erin George
Charles Huckelbury

ARTISTIC DIRECTOR
Elizabeth Calka

www.ingramcontent.com/pod-product-compliance
Lightning Source LLC
Chambersburg PA
CBHW032018290426
44109CB00013B/702